T0080382

GO BIRDING!

by

Captivate is published by Capstone Press, an imprint of Capstone.
1710 Roe Crest Drive, North Mankato, Minnesota 56003
www.capstonepub.com

Library of Congress Cataloging-in-Publication Data
Names: Garstecki, Julia, author.
Title: Go birding! / by Julia Garstecki.
Description: North Mankato, Minnesota : Capstone Press, [2022] |
Series: Wild Outdoors | Includes bibliographical references and index.
| Audience: Ages 8-11 | Audience: Grades 4-6 | Summary: "What was
that sound coming from the trees? Could it be a robin, a blue jay, or
even a woodpecker? Readers will sharpen their observation skills and
learn how to attract and tell the difference between many types of
birds"— Provided by publisher.
Identifiers: LCCN 2021002879 (print) | LCCN 2021002880 (ebook) |
ISBN 9781663905956 (hardcover) | ISBN 9781663920430 (paperback) |
ISBN 9781663905925 (pdf) | ISBN 9781663905949 (kindle edition)
Subjects: LCSH: Bird watching—Juvenile literature.
Classification: LCC QL677.5 .G365 2022 (print) | LCC QL677.5
(ebook) | DDC 598.072/34—dc23
LC record available at https://lccn.loc.gov/2021002879
LC ebook record available at https://lccn.loc.gov/202100288

Image Credits
iStockphoto: kali9, 29, robertcicchetti, 21; Newscom: akg-images, 27,
(bottom); Shutterstock: 4thebirds, 11, Agami Photo Agency, Cover,
Bonnie Taylor Barry, 22, Brian A Jackson, 17, (bottom right), Daboost,
17, (bottom left), Danita Delimont, 24, FotoRequest, 23, Gregory
Johnston, 20, Jakinnboaz, 12, Jessica2, 17, (bottom middle), Lakeview
Images, 9, Menno Schaefer, 5, Micah Watson, 27, (top), Michal Ninger,
15, Nadiia Korol, 16, Orla, 7, Pascal De Munck, 14, paula french, 6,
Pigprox, 1, Rochelle Rascon, 13, SanderMeertinsPhotography, 8,
TerraceStudio, 17, (top), Victor Suarez Naranjo, 19

Editorial Credits
Editor: Mandy Robbins; Designer: Jennifer Bergstrom; Media
Researcher: Morgan Walters; Production Specialist: Tori Abraham

Table of Contents

Words in **bold** are in the glossary.

Chapter 1

CALL OF THE WILD

You stand beside a tree, quiet as can be. Sun rays sparkle on the waves of a lake. Some of your friends page through their **field guides**. Others point to a tree. A large nest made of sticks rests high at the top. This is the spot! You wait.

A chirp-chirp-screech comes from above. You look toward the sound. The bird flying overhead is more beautiful and majestic than any photos you've seen. The bald eagle flaps its enormous wings. With its white head and tail, it soars gracefully overhead. Here comes another one. You cannot take your eyes off the birds. A few moments pass. No one has spoken. The eagles soar up and away. Though they're now out of sight, you feel you'll be connected to them forever.

A bald eagle in flight

Bird-watching, or birding, is a popular hobby. It is an activity that anyone can do, because birds are everywhere. And it's a low-cost hobby that gets you outside, which is good for your health. More people are discovering that birding is entertaining, relaxing, and can leave you feeling more connected to nature.

There are thousands of different kinds of birds to seek out. Ostriches in Africa look completely different than the penguins of Antarctica. Penguins look completely different than the white-headed Reeves pheasants of China.

An ostrich

Birds act as differently as they look. Certain cockatoos hit twigs against trees and make music. Flamingoes eat with their heads upside down. Some thrushes fart to move leaves in search of worms. Birding is the perfect way to spy on these intelligent and funny animals.

Ancient Ancestors

Have you ever thought that chickens looked like dinosaurs? Chickens and ostriches are the closest living things to dinosaurs. They are related to theropods. This group of dinosaurs included the Tyrannosaurus rex. Some theropods could fly. Over millions of years, these flying dinosaurs **evolved** to the chickens you see today.

A Tyrannosaurus rex

Chapter 2

EARLY BIRD OR NIGHT OWL?

The time of day you go birding matters. No matter where you are, you can see different birds at different times of the day. Have you heard the saying, "The early bird gets the worm?" Many birds are active at sunrise. That is when many insects are on the move. These creatures are often breakfast for a bird!

Eurasian reed warbler

Not all birds are early birds. Hawks are more active during the warmer parts of the day. If you want to see them, go out in the afternoon. And if you like to stay up late, you might be called a "night owl." This is because most owls hunt at night. Whether you are birding at sunrise or sunset, downtown or at a lake, your chances of seeing birds are excellent.

The morepork, New Zealand's native owl

The more you travel, the more kinds of birds
you'll see. Some birds, like pigeons, do well in
cities. In the wild, pigeons live on rocky cliffs.
Other birds, like ducks and herons, prefer water.

FACT

Not all owls are active at night and sleep during the day.
The northern hawk owl and the northern pygmy owl
sleep at night and are active during the day.

Chapter 3

LET'S GO BIRDING!

You can go birding anywhere at any time. But how will you know what you are looking at? A field guide will help you. A field guide is a book used to identify different kinds of birds. Field guides can be organized by bird size and shape or location.

Before birding, look through your field guide. Is there a particular bird you want to see? A field guide will tell you where you have the best chances of seeing it. For example, a ruby-throated hummingbird can be spotted in southern Canada and the northern United States in the summer months. In the winter months, hummingbirds travel to Mexico or Central America.

You can compare the photos of birds in your
field guide to those you see in nature.

Parts of Birds

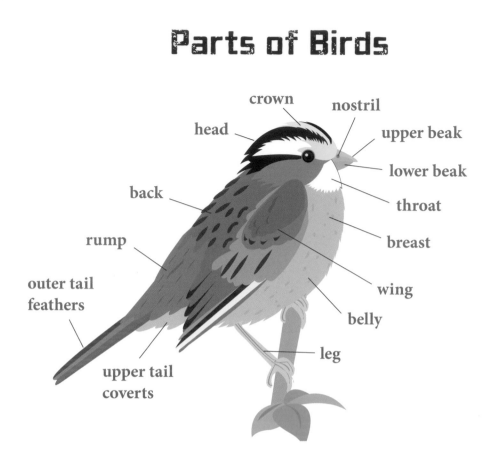

When you go birding, take a field guide and a trusted adult with you. **Observe** the birds. Notice the **markings** on different parts of their bodies. All birds have special markings on different parts of their bodies. The tip of the bird's head is the crown. Under the beak is the throat. Below that is the breast of the bird. There may be markings on the back, wings, and tail of the bird as well.

If you find a nest with eggs, mark the location. Then you can come back and watch the young birds hatch and grow up. But be careful not to disturb the nest or birds.

Along with your field guide, bring a pen and a notebook to keep notes. A camera is a great idea as well. Then, once your feathered friend has gone away, look back at your notes or photos. You can refer to the field guide to identify the bird.

A robin's eggs

A hummingbird sips nectar from a flower.

There are things you can do to improve your chances of seeing more birds. First, stay quiet. Noise will scare birds away. You might be surprised at how much you hear once you are silent. Birds will start to hop or sing. Woodpeckers will tap on the trees.

Look carefully. Where would a bird **perch** or hide? Look to tree branches, bushes, or a shoreline. Clumps of leaves or twigs might be a nest. Also, keep an eye on the sky. Which way are birds flying? Where did they come from? Good birders are observant and patient. The more you practice, the better trained you will be for noticing birds.

Once you've been birding a few times, you will notice things you may not have noticed before. For example, see how different birds' beaks can be.

Duck beaks, more commonly called bills, are long and spoon shaped. Bills crush food in the same way our teeth chew. The shape of a duck's bill is perfect for separating food from water.

The hummingbird's beak is long and narrow. It protects the bird's long tongue as it laps up **nectar** and water.

Woodpeckers have long, pointed beaks. They are perfect for drilling into trees. Woodpeckers use their beaks to look for bugs to eat.

A woodpecker pecks for insects in a tree trunk.

Binoculars are helpful when birding. Then you can watch a bird from afar without disturbing it. A light pair of binoculars is best. If you go birding for several hours, a light pair is easier to carry.

If you have a smartphone, download some birding apps. Apps such as the Audubon Bird Guide or Merlin Bird ID can help identify the birds you see. You could also take a picture of the bird and upload it on the app to identify it.

You can listen to bird songs on the app as well. Compare the app sounds to the bird you are hearing. Soon, you will know the call of a blue jay, the screech of an osprey, or the hoot of an owl!

BIRDING PACK LIST

- ☑ field guide
- ☑ binoculars
- ☑ weather-appropriate clothing
- ☑ camera/smartphone
- ☑ notebook and pens
- ☑ sturdy shoes
- ☑ sunscreen
- ☑ bug repellent
- ☑ hat

Chapter 4

WHERE TO FIND YOUR FEATHERED FRIENDS

Birding in the city can be very exciting! Rock pigeons, house sparrows, and European starlings do well in cities. But larger birds live in cities too. Berlin, Germany, is home to large populations of goshawks. These hawks feed on wild pigeons and rats. In fact, if you see pigeons anywhere, goshawks are likely to be nearby.

Kites are a type of bird that build their nests in trees in Delhi, India. Like goshawks, they feed on smaller birds and rats. Kites even help clean garbage off the streets! Many birders have begun studying **urban** birds like kites. They study how birds and people help each other.

A black kite in Dehli, India

Birds in South Africa also live in larger cities such as Cape Town. In fact, birding is a tourist attraction in the area. Yellow-billed egrets, kingfishers, and Cape sugarbirds are found there.

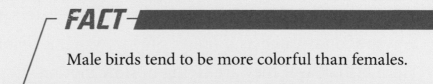

FACT

Male birds tend to be more colorful than females.

A blue heron soars through the air.

Water sources are a great place to go birding. One popular type of water bird is the heron. Herons are found almost anywhere there is water. Birders in Europe, North America, Asia, Africa, and Australia can study these long-legged beauties as they hunt in shallow waters. Once you spot one, watch as it hunts. Stay to watch it fly off. Herons look as if they are flying in slow motion.

Where there is water, there are likely ducks. Ducks are great for beginner birders to observe. If you've ever seen a duck with its back end in the air, you are seeing a **dabbler**. A mallard is a type of dabbler. Other ducks are diving ducks. They include the canvasback and redhead. They dive deep into the water. Eiders are the largest ducks in the Northern Hemisphere. They spend much of their time in icy Arctic waters.

Pale Male

Pale Male is one of the most famous red-tailed hawks of all time. He moved to Fifth Avenue in New York City around 1991. Pale Male made his nest in Central Park. Bird watchers named him for his uncommonly light-colored feathers. The dozens of red-tailed hawks spotted around the city are probably his children or grandchildren.

A red-tailed hawk in Central Park

A robin perches on a branch.

When birding in **rural** areas in the United States, you are more likely to come across downy woodpeckers. Other common birds found in many areas include robins, blue jays, and chickadees. You are more likely to hear these birds before you see them. Be still and listen carefully!

Experienced birders know tips to spot more birds. First, keep the sun behind you. This way birds will not appear shadowed. Not only will they be easier to see, but you'll get a better view of the birds' colors. Another trick good birders use is called pishing. Pishing is when a birder makes small kissing noises. It's quiet enough that the birds don't get scared, but they do get curious and want to explore the sound.

A blue jay sits on a tree limb.

**Two African goldfinches (top), an indigo
bunting (center), and a song sparrow (bottom)**

There may be times when an adult isn't able to take you birding. But you can still bring the birds to you! Different kinds of bird feeders attract different kinds of birds.

If you live in a city, an in-house window feeder is a good option. This plastic feeder sits on the windowsill. Rather than hanging outside your window, it actually curves into the house! You can also find bird feeders with suction cups that stick outside your windows. Once birds get comfortable with your bird feeder, you are likely to have regular visitors.

Different types of birds like different types of food. Bluebirds like mealworms. Blue jays prefer peanuts. The Eurasian nuthatch likes seeds. Orioles eat oranges. Hummingbirds drink sugar water. If you hang a thistle feeder filled with tiny bird seeds in your yard, you may see American or European goldfinches.

It can take some time for birds to find a new feeder. Birding takes patience sometimes, but it's worth the excitement when the birds come around.

Chapter 5

NEXT-LEVEL BIRDING

Birding is a growing hobby. Many parks and schools have bird-watching clubs. One of the best groups that teaches people about birding is the Audubon Society. This organization teaches people about the birds in their area. They often host birding events to teach bird-watching skills and help area birds. The Audubon Society works with other birding programs all over the world.

BirdLife International is another group trying to help birds. It has branches in more than 100 countries. The group's goal is to **conserve** birds and their **habitats**. Birders all over the world help BirdLife track bird populations. They learn what helps and hurts birds. Then they can teach others what they know.

James Audubon: Inspiring Others

John James Audubon

John James Audubon is one of the best-known birders. He went by James and was born in 1785. Audubon was passionate about birds and art. He painted birds as true to life as he could. He wanted to capture the images of birds so that others could enjoy their beauty. He inspired others to explore nature, especially birds. The Audubon Society is named for him.

Being a birder is also a responsibility. It's important to practice good birding habits. Never cause damage to a bird habitat. If you are lucky enough to see eggs in a nest or baby birds, leave them alone. Also, keep in mind a mother bird might be waiting to come back to the nest to feed her babies. You might be scaring her away.

If you hang bird feeders, keep them clean. Hang them where it will be safest for birds. A few feet away from trees or bushes is a good spot. The birds can quickly fly back to the tree if they get scared.

Birding is a rewarding hobby that can be done by anyone anywhere. The more we watch the birds, the more we notice other aspects of nature. Because birding can help us feel more connected to nature, the hobby inspires many of us to protect it. The more we can keep the environment safe for the birds, the more birds we'll have to enjoy.

GLOSSARY

conserve (kuhn-SURV)—to save

dabbler (DAB-lurh)—a duck that dabs it head underwater to trap food

evolve (ih-VAHLV)—for a type of animal to change over time from one species to another

field guide (FEELD GIDE)—a book for the identification of birds, flowers, minerals, or other things in their natural environment

habitat (HAB-uh-tat)—the natural place and conditions in which a plant or animal lives

marking (MAR-king)—a patch of color or pattern of marks on fur, feathers, or skin

nectar (NEK-tur)—sweet liquid found in many flowers

observe (ub-SERV)—to watch someone or something closely in order to learn something

perch (PERCH)—for a bird to find a high place where it can rest and view its surroundings

rural (RUR-uhl)—of the countryside; away from cities and towns

urban (UR-buhn)—having to do with a city

READ MORE

Alderfer, Jonathan, and Noah Stryker. *National Geographic Kids Backyard Guide to the Birds of North America.* Washington, D.C.: National Geographic, 2019.

DeWitz, Karen. *Look at that Bird! A Young Naturalist's Guide to Pacific Northwest Birding.* Seattle: Sasquatch Books, 2021.

Wolfson, Elisa, and Margaret Barker. *Audubon Birding Adventures for Kids: Activities and Ideas for Watching, Feeding, and Housing Our Feathered Friends.* Beverley, MA: Cool Springs Press, 2020.

INTERNET SITES

All About Birds
allaboutbirds.org/cams/all-cams/

The Kid Should See This: The Cornell Lab of Ornithology's Bird Song Hero
thekidshouldseethis.com/post/the-cornell-lab-of-ornithologys-bird-song-hero

National Geographic Kids: Birds
kids.nationalgeographic.com/animals/birds/

INDEX